Plus

President
Donald
Trump

by Nick Robison

T0044792

CAPSTONE PRESS
a capstone imprint

Pebble Plus is published by Capstone Press,
1710 Roe Crest Drive, North Mankato, Minnesota 56003
www.mycapstone.com

Library of Congress Cataloging-in-Publication Data
Cataloging-in-publication information is on file with the Library of Congress.
ISBN 978-1-5157-7895-0 (hardcover)
ISBN 978-1-5157-7896-7 (paperback)
ISBN 978-1-5157-7897-4 (eBook PDF)

Editorial Credits
Jessica Nelson, designer; Scott Burger, media researcher

Photo Credits
AP Photo: Mike Groll, 7; Getty Images: New York Daily News Archive, 11, Stringer/Amanda Edwards, 15, Stringer/Kena
Betancur, cover; Library of Congress: 29 (all); Newscom: AdMedia/CNP/Ron Sachs, 21, Reuters/Brendan McDermid, 17, Sipa
USA/Anthony Behar, 27, ZUMA Press/Judie Burstein, 5; Shutterstock: Christopher Halloran, 19, Evan El-Amin, 1, jiawangkun,
13, Joseph Sohm, 23, Lev Radin, 25, SINITAR, 9

Note to Parents and Teachers

President Donald Trump supports national history standards related to people and culture. The images
support early readers in understanding the text. The repetition of words and phrases helps early
readers learn new words. This book also introduces early readers to subject-specific vocabulary words,
which are defined in the Glossary section. Early readers may need assistance to read some words and
to use the Table of Contents, Glossary, Read More, Internet Sites, and Index sections of the book.

Printed in the United States of America.
010249S17

Table of Contents

Born into Business

Donald Trump was born in

New York City on June 14, 1946.

He was the fourth of five children.

Donald's father, Frederick,

ran a company that built

apartment buildings. His mother,

Mary, worked with various charities.

born in New York City

1946

Donald (center) with his father, Frederick, and his mother, Mary

When he was 13, Donald's parents sent him to a military school in New York. The school helped Donald set and reach goals. He also enjoyed playing baseball, soccer, and other sports at the school.

born in New York City

1946   1959

attends the New York Military Academy

Donald in the 1964 yearbook from the New York Military Academy

DONALD JOHN TRUMP
"D. T."
Jamaica, New York

After military school, Donald

went to Fordham University in

New York. Later he went to

the Wharton School of the

University of Pennsylvania.

In 1968, Donald earned a

college degree in economics.

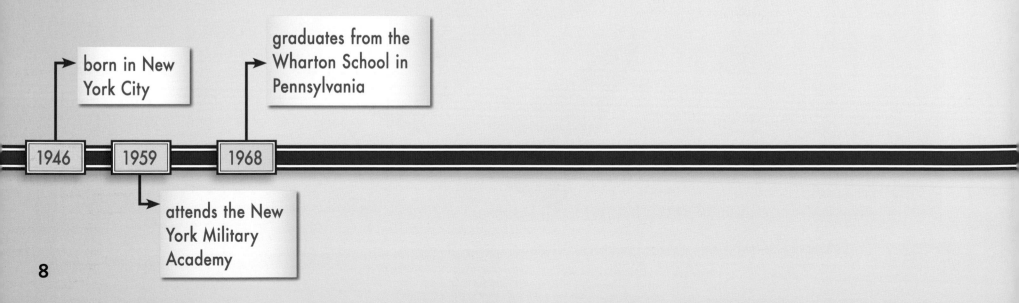

born in New
York City

graduates from the
Wharton School in
Pennsylvania

1946

1959

1968

attends the New
York Military
Academy

the Wharton School in Pennsylvania

The Business World

In 1971, Donald took over his father's business. Soon he renamed it The Trump Organization. He bought, sold, and constructed many buildings. These included office buildings, hotels, and resorts. Donald earned a lot of money.

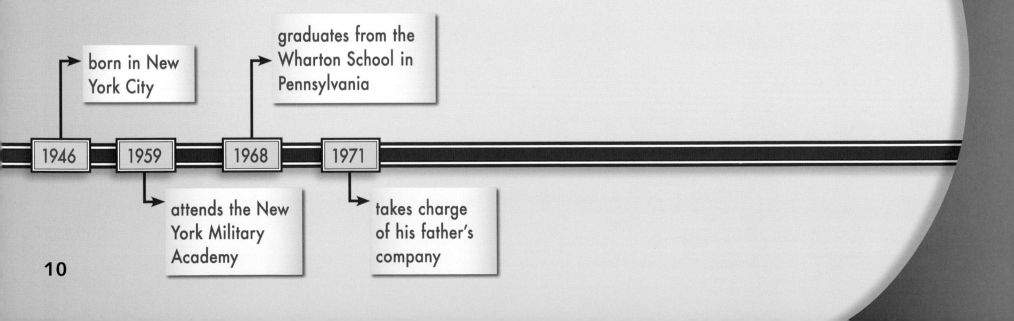

born in New York City

graduates from the Wharton School in Pennsylvania

1946   1959   1968   1971

attends the New York Military Academy

takes charge of his father's company

Donald announces plans for a convention center in New York in 1977.

Donald owns many fancy buildings in the United States and around the world. Many of the buildings have his last name on them. Donald has also written several books about business and his life.

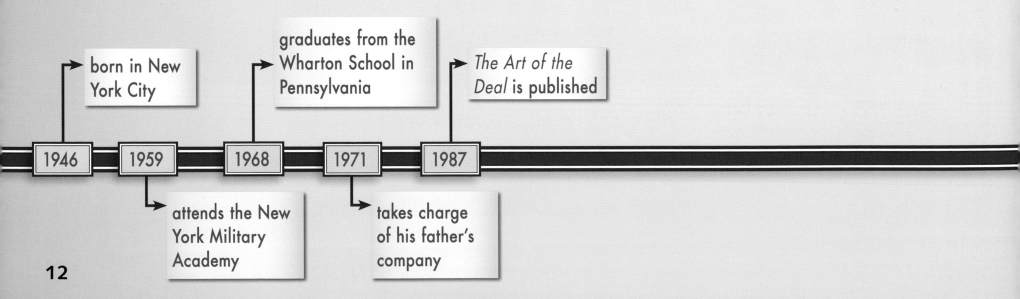

graduates from the Wharton School in Pennsylvania

born in New York City

The Art of the Deal is published

1946 1959 1968 1971 1987

attends the New York Military Academy

takes charge of his father's company

the main entrance to Trump Tower on Fifth Avenue in New York City

Donald also became a
famous entertainer.
He starred in his own reality
TV show, *The Apprentice*.
In the show, people tried to win
a job working for Donald.

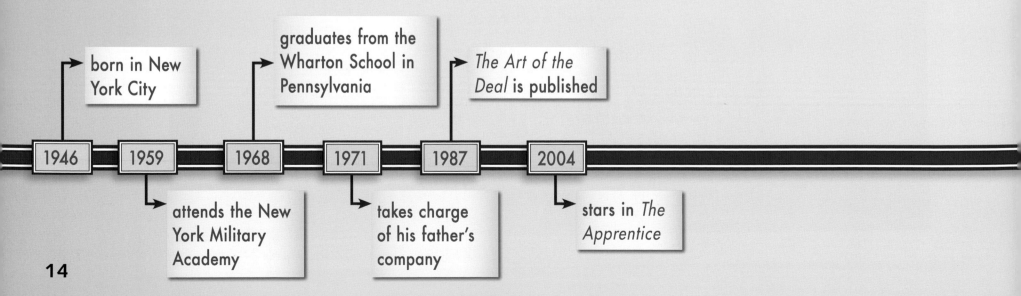

born in New
York City

graduates from the
Wharton School in
Pennsylvania

*The Art of the
Deal* is published

1946   1959   1968   1971   1987   2004

attends the New
York Military
Academy

takes charge
of his father's
company

stars in *The
Apprentice*

Family Life

Donald Trump has been married three times.

He has five children.

He married his current wife, Melania, in 2005.

She used to be a model.

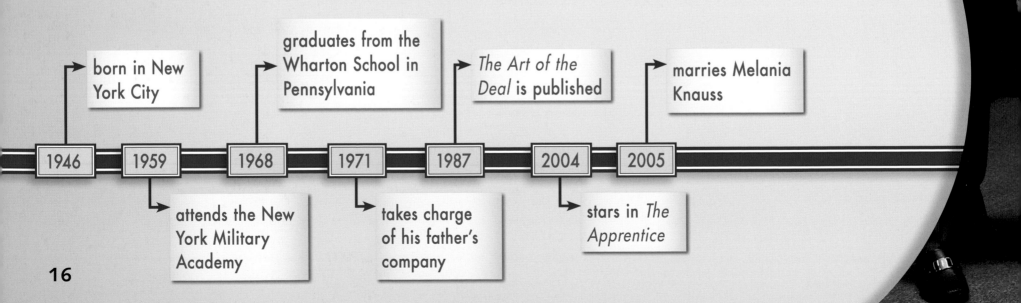

| 1946 | 1959 | 1968 | 1971 | 1987 | 2004 | 2005 |

born in New York City

graduates from the Wharton School in Pennsylvania

The Art of the Deal is published

marries Melania Knauss

attends the New York Military Academy

takes charge of his father's company

stars in *The Apprentice*

Donald Trump with his family

Change to Politics

Over time, Donald became

interested in politics.

He thought about running

for president several times.

He also thought about

running for governor of

New York in 2006 and 2014.

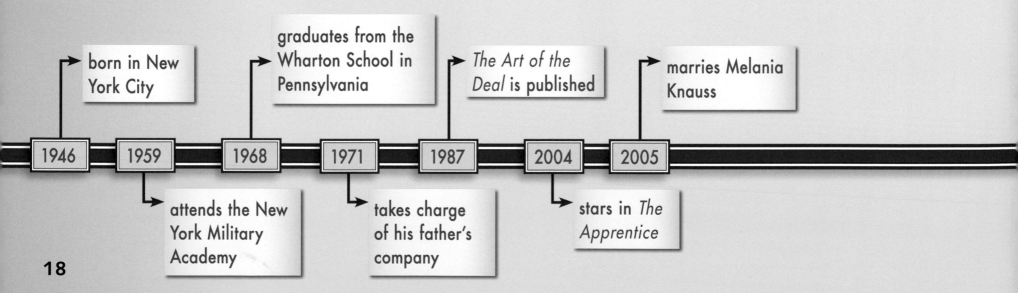

| 1946 | 1959 | 1968 | 1971 | 1987 | 2004 | 2005 |

born in New York City

attends the New York Military Academy

graduates from the Wharton School in Pennsylvania

takes charge of his father's company

The Art of the Deal is published

stars in *The Apprentice*

marries Melania Knauss

Donald ran for president in 2016 as a Republican candidate. He had never held a political position before. He formed a team to help him win the campaign.

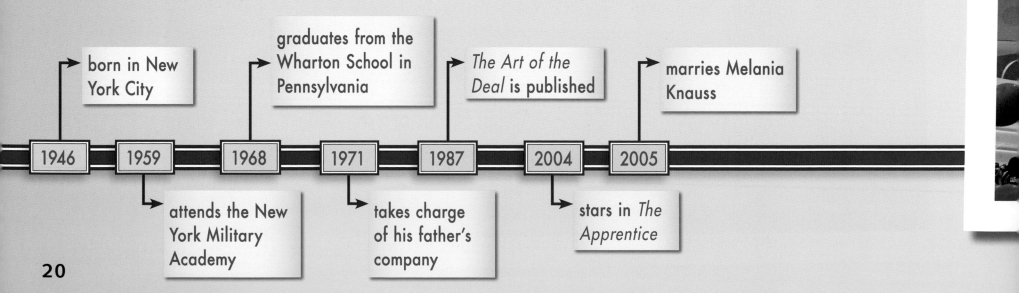

| 1946 | 1959 | 1968 | 1971 | 1987 | 2004 | 2005 |

born in New York City

graduates from the Wharton School in Pennsylvania

The Art of the Deal is published

marries Melania Knauss

attends the New York Military Academy

takes charge of his father's company

stars in *The Apprentice*

In July 2016, Donald Trump became the Republican presidential candidate.

Donald talked about making
more jobs available for workers.
He also covered health care,
keeping Americans safe,
and many other topics.
People were excited about the
changes he planned to make.

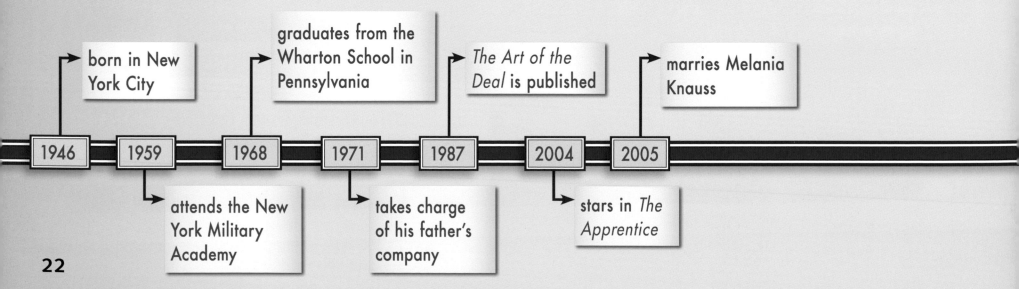

born in New
York City

graduates from the
Wharton School in
Pennsylvania

*The Art of the
Deal* is published

marries Melania
Knauss

| 1946 | 1959 | 1968 | 1971 | 1987 | 2004 | 2005 |

attends the New
York Military
Academy

takes charge
of his father's
company

stars in *The
Apprentice*

Winning the Election

Americans voted on November 8, 2016. The next day, it was announced that Donald had won the election. He gave an acceptance speech in New York. The large crowd chanted, "USA! USA!"

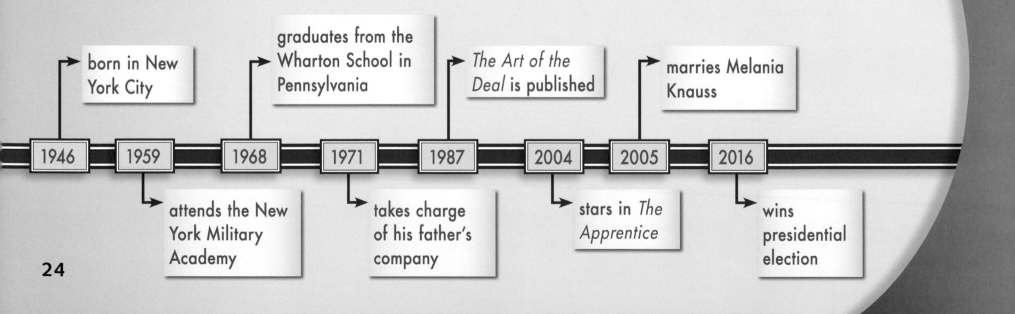

| 1946 | 1959 | 1968 | 1971 | 1987 | 2004 | 2005 | 2016 |

born in New York City

attends the New York Military Academy

graduates from the Wharton School in Pennsylvania

takes charge of his father's company

The Art of the Deal is published

stars in *The Apprentice*

marries Melania Knauss

wins presidential election

Donald gives a victory speech next to his wife, Melania, and son Barron.

President Trump

Donald Trump became the 45th president on January 20, 2017. His slogan during the campaign was "Make America Great Again." Americans are excited to see what Donald can do to make that happen.

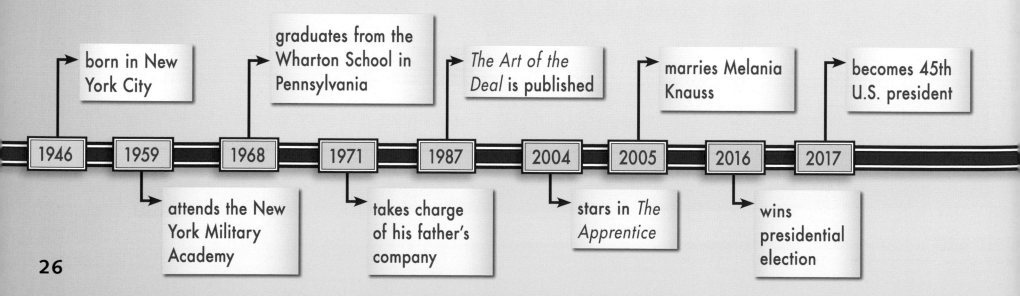

1946 — born in New York City

1959 — attends the New York Military Academy

1968 — graduates from the Wharton School in Pennsylvania

1971 — takes charge of his father's company

1987 — *The Art of the Deal* is published

2004 — stars in *The Apprentice*

2005 — marries Melania Knauss

2016 — wins presidential election

2017 — becomes 45th U.S. president

Donald Trump is sworn in as the 45th president of the United States.

Facts about Donald Trump

Born:
June 14, 1946

Parents:
Frederick and Mary Trump

Marriages:
Ivana Zelníčková (1977–1992)
Marla Maples (1993–1999)
Melania Knauss (2005–present)

Children:
Donald Jr., born in 1977 (with Ivana Zelníčková)
Ivanka, born in 1981 (with Ivana Zelníčková)
Eric, born in 1984 (with Ivana Zelníčková)
Tiffany, born in 1993 (with Marla Maples)
Barron, born in 2006 (with Melania Knauss)

Favorite movies:
Donald has many favorite movies,
including *Citizen Kane* and *The Godfather*

Favorite sport:
Golf

Nickname:
The Donald

Presidents of the United States

George Washington, 1789–1797
John Adams, 1797–1801
Thomas Jefferson, 1801–1809
James Madison, 1809–1817
James Monroe, 1817–1825
John Quincy Adams, 1825–1829
Andrew Jackson, 1829–1837
Martin Van Buren, 1837–1841
William Henry Harrison, 1841
John Tyler, 1841–1845
James K. Polk, 1845–1849
Zachary Taylor, 1849–1850
Millard Fillmore, 1850–1853
Franklin Pierce, 1853–1857
James Buchanan, 1857–1861
Abraham Lincoln, 1861–1865
Andrew Johnson, 1865–1869
Ulysses S. Grant, 1869–1877
Rutherford B. Hayes, 1877–1881
James A. Garfield, 1881
Chester Arthur, 1881–1885

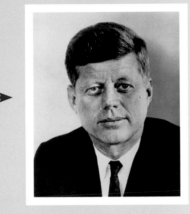

Grover Cleveland, 1885–1889
Benjamin Harrison, 1889–1893
Grover Cleveland, 1893–1897
William McKinley, 1897–1901
Theodore Roosevelt, 1901–1909
William H. Taft, 1909–1913
Woodrow Wilson, 1913–1921
Warren G. Harding, 1921–1923
Calvin Coolidge, 1923–1929
Herbert Hoover, 1929–1933
Franklin D. Roosevelt, 1933–1945
Harry S. Truman, 1945–1953
Dwight D. Eisenhower, 1953–1961
John F. Kennedy, 1961–1963
Lyndon B. Johnson, 1963–1969
Richard M. Nixon, 1969–1974
Gerald R. Ford, 1974–1977
Jimmy Carter, 1977–1981
Ronald Reagan, 1981–1989
George H. W. Bush, 1989–1993
William J. Clinton, 1993–2001
George W. Bush, 2001–2009
Barack Obama, 2009–2017
Donald Trump, 2017–

Glossary

acceptance speech—a speech a politician gives when he or she wins an election

campaign—actions and events done with a specific goal, such as an election

candidate—a person who runs for office, such as president

charity—a group that helps people in need

construct—to build

election—the act of choosing someone or deciding something by voting

governor—a person elected to be the head of a state's government

reality TV—a TV show without any scripts or professional actors

vote—to make a choice in an election

Read More

Lewison, Wendy Cheyette. *P Is for President*. New York: Grosset & Dunlap, 2016.

Stier, Catherine. *If I Ran for President*. New York: AV2 by Weigl, 2013.

Stine, Megan. *Where Is the White House?* New York: Grosset & Dunlap, 2015.

Internet Sites

FactHound offers a safe, fun way to find Internet sites related to this book. All of the sites on FactHound have been researched by our staff.

Here's all you do:

Visit *www.facthound.com*

Type in this code: 9781515778950

Super-cool stuff! Check out projects, games and lots more at **www.capstonekids.com**

Index